John Foster and Korky Paul

DINOSAUR
POEMS

Oxford University Press

Oxford New York Toronto

1

Acknowledgements

The editor and publisher are grateful for permission to include the following copyright material.

Tony Bradman, 'At the Museum'. © 1993 Tony Bradman. Reprinted by permission of Rogers, Coleridge, & White Ltd.

John Cotton, 'The Bookoceros or Ancient Thesaurus'. © 1993 John Cotton. Reprinted by permission of the author.

Max Fatchen, 'Who's There?'. © 1993 Max Fatchen. Reprinted by permission of John Johnson (Authors' Agent) Ltd.

John Foster, 'Ten Dancing Dinosaurs'. © 1993 John Foster. Reprinted by permission of the author.

David Harmer, 'Dinosaur Stomp' from *My Blue Poetry Book* (Macmillan Educational), edited Moira Andrew. Reprinted by permission of the author.

Trevor Harvey, 'At the Dinosaurs' Party'. © 1993 Trevor Harvey. Reprinted by permission of the author.

Gail Kredenser, 'Brontosaurus'. © Gail Kredenser. Used with permission.

Wendy Larmont, 'Stegosaurus'. © 1993 Wendy Larmont. Reprinted by permission of the author.

Doug MacLeod, 'Ode to an Extinct Dinosaur' from *In the Garden of Bad Things*. Reprinted by permission of Penguin Books Australia Ltd as publisher.

Wes Magee, 'Tyrannosaurus Rex'. © Wes Magee. Reprinted by permission of the author.

Trevor Millum, 'A Stegosaurus is for life'. © 1993 Trevor Millum. Reprinted by permission of the author.

Brian Moses, 'Trouble at the Dinosaur Café'. © 1993 Brian Moses. Reprinted by permission of the author.

Judith Nicholls, 'Dinosauristory', first published in *Popcorn Pie* by Judith Nicholls (Mary Glasgow Publications), © Judith Nicholls 1988. Reprinted by permission of the author.

Jack Prelutsky, 'Ankylosaurus' from *Tyrannosaurus Was a Beast*. Text © 1988 by Jack Prelutsky. Published in the UK by Walker Books Limited and reprinted with their permission. Published in the USA by Wm Morrow & Co. Inc.

Irene Rawnsley, 'James and the Dinosaur'. © 1993 Irene Rawnsley. Reprinted by permission of the author.

Charles Thomson, 'My Pet Dinosaur' from *I'm Brilliant* (Collins Book Bus). Reprinted by permission of the author and Collins Educational Publ.

Clive Webster, 'Companion' and 'Problem Solved' both © 1993 Clive Webster. Reprinted by permission of the author.

Martyn Wiley, 'When the Dinosaur Came to Stay'. © 1993 Martyn Wiley. Reprinted by permission of the author.

Raymond Wilson, 'The Big Con'. © 1993 Raymond Wilson. Reprinted by permission of the author.

We may have failed in some instances to contact the copyright holder. If notified, the publisher will be pleased to make necessary corrections in future editions.

For Angus Hamilton Gordon   K.P.

Oxford University Press, Walton Street, Oxford OX2 6DP

Oxford New York Toronto
Delhi Bombay Calcutta Madras Karachi
Kuala Lumpur Singapore Hong Kong Tokyo
Nairobi Dar es Salaam Cape Town
Melbourne Auckland Madrid

and associated companies in
Berlin Ibadan

Oxford is a trade mark of Oxford University Press

This selection and arrangement © John Foster 1993

Illustrations © Korky Paul 1993

First published 1993
First published in this paperback edition 1994

Reprinted 1994

Hardback ISBN 0 19 276095 5
Paperback ISBN 0 19 276126 9

A CIP catalogue reference for this book is available from the British Library

Set by Pentacor PLC, High Wycombe, Bucks
Printed in Hong Kong

CONTENTS

Companion

I have an allosaurus
And I take him everywhere,
And really I can't understand
Why people stop and stare.

He's loving, kind and gentle,
He wouldn't hurt a soul,
Unless of course you laughed at him—
And then he'd eat you whole!

Clive Webster

4

Dinosaur Stomp

I thought I saw
a Dinosaur
buy a pair of slippers
in a big shoe-store
I asked him what
he bought them for
and he told me
his paw was sore
and what's more
began to roar
and showed me what
his teeth were for.

I ran like mad
across the floor
and bolted through
the shoe-store door
and nevermore
no nevermore
laughed out loud
at a Dinosaur.

David Harmer

Ten Dancing Dinosaurs

Ten dancing dinosaurs in a chorus line
One fell and split her skirt, then there were nine.

Nine dancing dinosaurs at a village fête
One was raffled as a prize, then there were eight.

Seven dancing dinosaurs performing magic tricks
One did a vanishing act, then there were six.

Six dancing dinosaurs
Learning how to jive

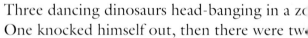

Four dancing dinosaurs waltzing in the sea
A mermaid kidnapped one, then there were three.

Three dancing dinosaurs head-banging in a zo
One knocked himself out, then there were tw

Eight dancing dinosaurs on a pier in Devon
One fell overboard, then there were seven.

One got twisted in a knot,
Then there were five.

Five dancing dinosaurs gyrating on the floor
One crashed through the floorboards, then there were four.

wo dancing dinosaurs rocking round the sun
ne collapsed from sunstroke, then there was one.

One dancing dinosaur hijacked a plane
Flew off to Alaska and was never seen again.

John Foster

7

Stegosaurus

I have a stegosaurus
He's really rather sweet.
But he's very, very fussy
About the food he'll eat.

I offered him a burger,
A plate of egg and chips,
A dish of chicken curry,
But none would pass his lips.

I asked, 'What would be tasty?
I'll get it if I can.'
He said, 'I'd better tell you . . .
I'm a VEGETARIAN!'

Wendy Larmont

Dinosauristory

Hocus, pocus,
plodding through the swamp;
I'm a diplodocus,
chomp, chomp, chomp!
Grass for breakfast,
I could eat a tree!
Grass for lunch and dinner
and grass for tea.
I'm a diplodocus
plodding through the swamp,
hocus-rocus pocus,
chomp, chomp, chomp!

Judith Nicholls

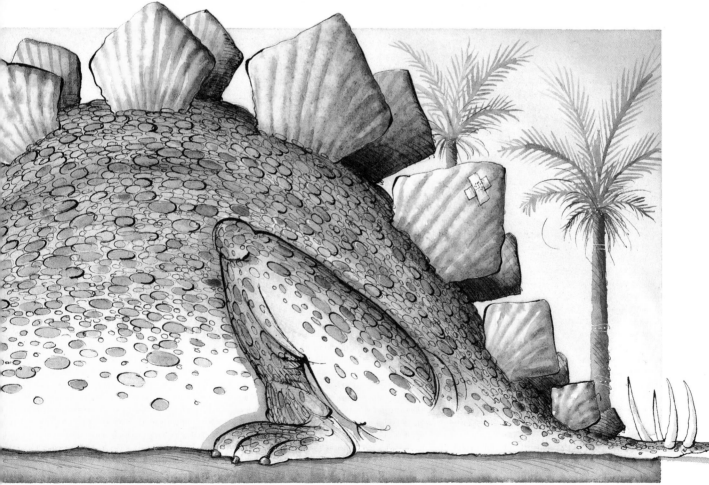

Tyrannosaurus Rex
(the King of the tyrant lizards)

Two daft little arms like toasting forks,
enough skin to make coats for ten men.
  As dirty as pitch
  (he slept rough in a ditch),
and the feet from a monstrous hen.

A bit of a freak—part beast, part bird.
Would you dare stick your tongue out at him?
  He's a mean dinosaur
  with a mouth wide as a door
and teeth that stand up dagger-slim.

Across the mud flats he belts in top gear;
a rogue lighthouse with blood on his brain.
  Better kneel down and pray
  for all those in his way:
he'll grind bones again and again.

Wes Magee

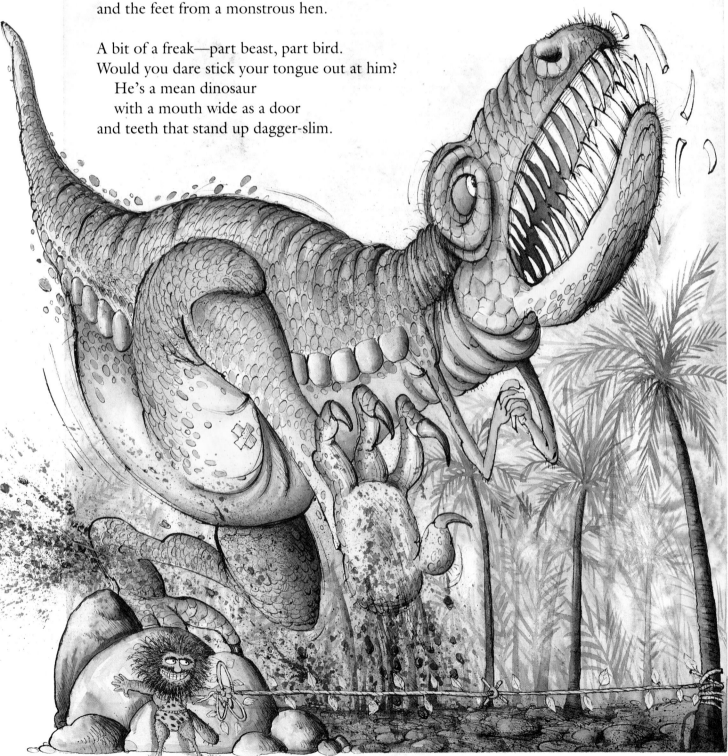

10

Ankylosaurus

Clankity Clankity Clankity Clank!
Ankylosaurus was built like a tank,
its hide was a fortress as sturdy as steel,
it tended to be an inedible meal.

It was armoured in front, it was armoured behind,
there wasn't a thing on its miniscule mind,
it waddled about on its four stubby legs,
nibbling on plants with a mouthful of pegs.

Ankylosaurus was best left alone,
its tail was a cudgel of gristle and bone,
Clankity Clankity Clankity Clank!
Ankylosaurus was built like a tank.

Jack Prelutsky

Ode to an Extinct Dinosaur

Iguanadon, I loved you,
With all your spiky scales,
Your massive jaws,
Impressive claws
And teeth like horseshoe nails.

Iguanadon, I loved you.
It moved me close to tears
When first I read
That you've been dead
For ninety million years.

Doug Macleod

The Bookoceros or Ancient Thesaurus

The Thesaurus has a ravenous appetite
From any passing page he will take a bite.
As for dictionaries and such
He eats them for breakfast
He likes them so much.

Nouns are his staple as you would guess
Though he's not averse to a well-cooked mess
Of a porridge of paragraphs containing long words,
But he prefers prepositions with a few stewed verbs.

If he should over-eat, what will he do?
He will just cough up a sentence or two!

John Cotton

The Big Con

Brontosaurus, Stegosaurus, whatever the name;
Tyrannosaurus, Spinosaurus, it's one and the same—
They clubbed together, one and all,
To make the rest of us look *small*!

As long as a cricket pitch, snout to tail,
With tree-trunk legs and plated mail,
Snarling like thunder, and humped like a hill,
They could eat a whole haystack and be hungry still.

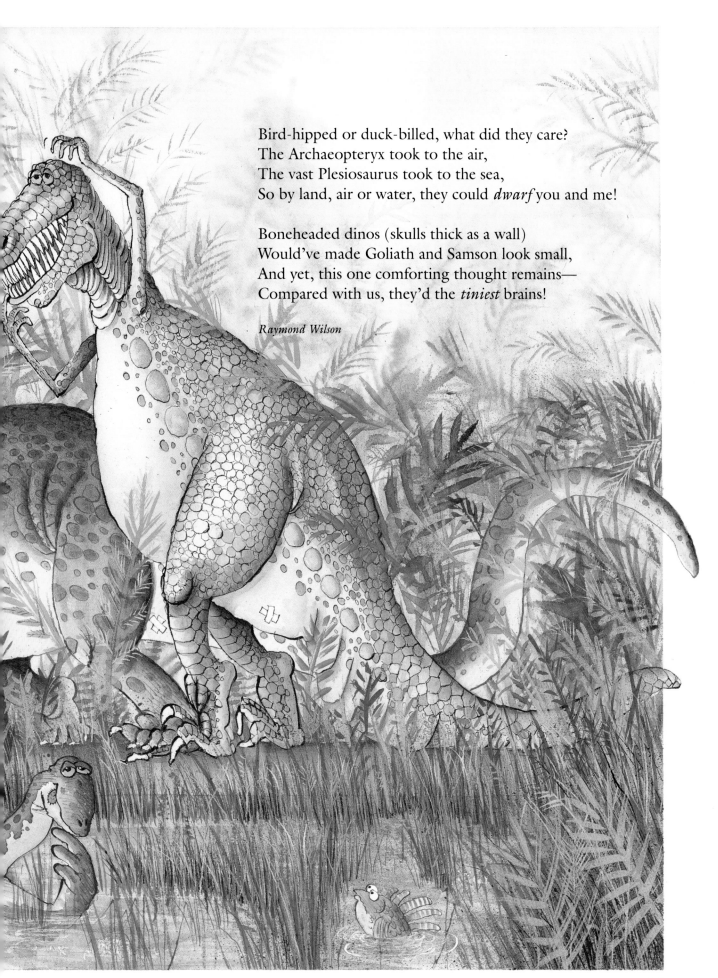

Bird-hipped or duck-billed, what did they care?
The Archaeopteryx took to the air,
The vast Plesiosaurus took to the sea,
So by land, air or water, they could *dwarf* you and me!

Boneheaded dinos (skulls thick as a wall)
Would've made Goliath and Samson look small,
And yet, this one comforting thought remains—
Compared with us, they'd the *tiniest* brains!

Raymond Wilson

Brontosaurus

The giant brontosaurus
Was a prehistoric chap
With four fat feet to stand on
And a very skimpy lap.
The scientists assure us
Of a most amazing thing—
A brontosaurus blossomed
When he had a chance to sing!

(The bigger brontosauruses,
Who liked to sing in choruses,
Would close their eyes and harmonize
And sing most anything.)

They growled and they yowled,
They deedled and they dummed;
They warbled and they whistled,
They howled and they hummed.
They didn't eat, they didn't sleep;
They sang and sang all day.
Now all you'll find are footprints
Where they tapped the time away!

Gail Kredenser

At the Dinosaurs' Party

At the dinosaurs' party
They had a great time—
They played HEAVY ROCK
And then ROLLED in the slime!

They kept a GOOD BEAT
With a SWISH of the tail,
As they ROARED up and down
The REPTILEAN scale!

At the dinosaurs' party
They SHOOK the whole earth—
As they RANTED and RAVED
For ALL THEY WERE WORTH!

Trevor Harvey

Trouble at the Dinosaur Café

Down at the dinosaur café
everybody was doing fine.
Steggy was slurping swamp juice
while Iggy sat down to dine.

Bronto was eating his tree-roots
and had ordered vegetable pie,
when in stomped Tyrannosaurus
with a wicked gleam in his eye.

He read the menu from left to right
then gobbled it up in one gulp.
He chewed upon it thoughtfully
while the paper turned to pulp.

'You plant eaters are fine,' he said,
'if that's all you want to eat.
But I'm a growing dinosaur
and my stomach cries out for meat.'

'I need something extra
to see me through my day.
I do lots of ROARING and BELLOWING,
I just can't get by on hay.'

Steggy stiffened, Iggy trembled,
while Bronto fell off his chair.
Tyrannosaurus turned his head
and fixed him with his stare.

'There's nothing I like more,' he said,
'than a tasty dinosaur stew,
and for extra special flavour
I'll add YOU and YOU and YOU . . . !'

Brian Moses

When the Dinosaur Came to Stay

Monday; he got stuck in the bath.
We had to get a crane
To pull him out.

Tuesday; he sat on the settee
It broke into a thousand bits
Mum shouted at him.

Wednesday; he went into the garden
Ate all the roses
Then started chewing the lawn.

Thursday; he helped in the kitchen
Peeled three tons of potatoes
Then pulled the taps off the wall.

Friday; the water was two metres deep
So he sucked it out of the house
Sprayed it down the street.

Saturday; he went home, caught a bus
Picked it up in one hand, had a look inside
Then caught the train instead.

Martyn Wiley

My Dinosaur's Day in the Park

My pet dinosaur got in trouble
When we went for a walk in the park.
I took off his leash and let him run free.
He didn't come back until dark.
He ate up the new row of oak trees
(The gardener was fit to be tied).
Then he stopped in the playground and bent down his head
And the kids used his neck for a slide.

He knocked down the fence by the boat pond
With a swing of his twenty-foot tail;
When he stopped to explain he was sorry,
His legs blocked the bicycle trail.

When the sun set, my dino got worried;
He's always been scared of the dark.
He sat down on the ground and started to cry,
His tears flooded out the whole park.
A friend of mine rowed his boat over
When he heard of my pet dino's sad roar.
He showed him the way home to my house
And helped him unlock the front door.

He's a lovable, lumbering fellow
But after my pet had his spree,
They put up a sign in the park and it reads
NO DINOS ALLOWED TO RUN FREE.

Elizabeth Winthrop Mahoney

A Stegosaurus is for Life

Down in a fern-decked valley
Far from the sun's fierce glare,
A smiling stegosaurus
Laid her eggs with loving care.

But so as to protect them
From tyrannosaurus rex,
She thought, *I'll dig a little hole*
And cover up these eggs.

The soil around was rich and moist;
The hole she dug was deep.
The fine pink eggs they huddled there,
As if they were asleep.

Now Mrs Steg was charming
And kind to all she met
But she had one tiny little fault:
She was likely to forget.

So time went by and seasons passed,
An ice-age came and went.
The eggs lay frozen in the earth
Near Tenterden in Kent.

One day a yellow JCB
Laying pipelines for some gas,
Dug up five strange pink objects
And laid them in the grass.

X Y and Zeddy saw them;
They took them home as toys
And in the middle of the night
They heard a tapping noise.

At first a claw crept through the crack
Fast followed by a snout,
A head and then a body
As a grey green . . . *thing* hatched out.

The children were delighted;
They took them out for walks.
They fed them on bananas
And dandelion stalks.

The children grew up slowly:
The stegosauri grew up fast.
Their tails all sprouted deadly spikes
And their bony plates were vast.

'They'll have to go!' said grown-ups,
'To Science Lab—or zoo—
It might be to a circus—
It's really up to you.'

*WANTED: good home for a reptile.
As watchdogs they're the best,
They'll baby-sit for hours
And stamp on household pests;
Make all your neighbours jealous
Of your rockeries on legs
They'll scare a burglar silly
And may even lay you eggs!*

Trevor Millum

My Pet Dinosaur

My dinosaur
was getting thinner
and so I brought him
home for dinner.

He ate as fast
as he was able:
he ate the food,
he ate the table.

He ate the fridge,
he ate the chair,
he ate my favourite
teddy bear.

He is a very
naughty pet.
He even ate
the TV set.

Charles Thomson

Who's There?

If you hear a dinosaur
Knocking loudly on your door,
Through the keyhole firmly say
'Nobody is home today'.
If the bell should start to ring,
Tell the beast, 'No visiting'.
If you see there's more than one,
Turn around and start to run.

Max Fatchen

At the Museum

I was an ancient dinosaur
   I lived so long ago;
I walked through steaming jungles
   And my gait was very slow.

I ate the juicy fern plants
   And I wallowed in the mud;
I loved to lie out in the sun
   And feel it warm my blood.

I splashed along the sea-shore
   I squelched in muddy swamps,
And when I crossed the boiling plains
   My feet went . . .
STOMP! STOMP STOMP!

My giant footsteps shook the Earth,
   My shadow terrified
The tiny, waiting creatures
   Who watched me as I died.

I was a meal for others
   As the skin fell from my bones . . .
A hundred million years went by.
   My bones turned into stone.

A fossil remnant I became,
   Some bones locked in the land,
And there I stayed till I was freed
   And cleaned by human hands.

My bones were put together
   To make a fine display,
And you can come to look at me
   Almost every day.

Come closer . . . can you feel it?
   It's the jungle's steaming heat.
And now the ground starts shaking
   As I walk with giant feet.

See the fern trees parting
   As thunderous and slow
I come looking for my dinner . . .
   But that was long ago.

I was an ancient dinosaur,
   But now you find me here;
A message that's been waiting
   For a hundred million years.

Tony Bradman

James and the Dinosaur

At the Museum
when the keeper couldn't see him
James climbed inside the bones
of a dinosaur.

Up its tail
through the rib rings
James explored its crevices
put his head into the skull,
imagining.

Quick heart
hot breath
such questionings inside him
made the bones of the dinosaur
erupt from death.

He tore at his moorings
pushed aside the keeper
broke from the stares
of the people come to see;
smashed through the wall
with James riding inside him
crashed into the street
to be free.

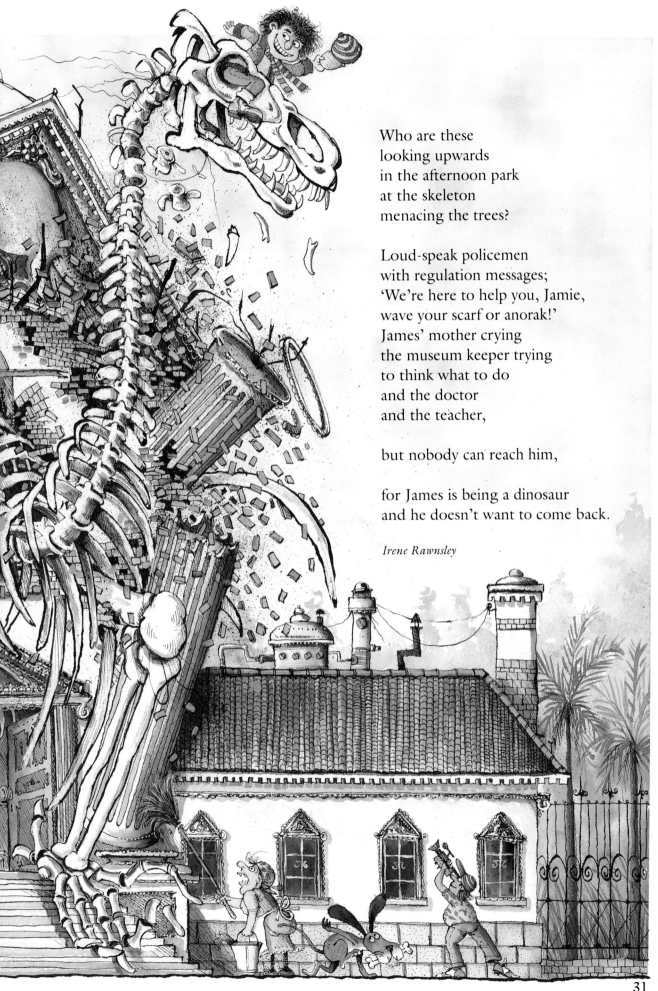

Who are these
looking upwards
in the afternoon park
at the skeleton
menacing the trees?

Loud-speak policemen
with regulation messages;
'We're here to help you, Jamie,
wave your scarf or anorak!'
James' mother crying
the museum keeper trying
to think what to do
and the doctor
and the teacher,

but nobody can reach him,

for James is being a dinosaur
and he doesn't want to come back.

Irene Rawnsley

Problem Solved

Our teacher says it's a mystery
Why dinosaurs died long ago.
They just disappeared
After millions of years
And why, we may well never know.

But I've got a theory about it—
They didn't just run out of breath.
Like us they had schools
With lessons and rules
And the teachers just bored them to death.

Clive Webster